The
GUITAR
CHORD
Dictionary

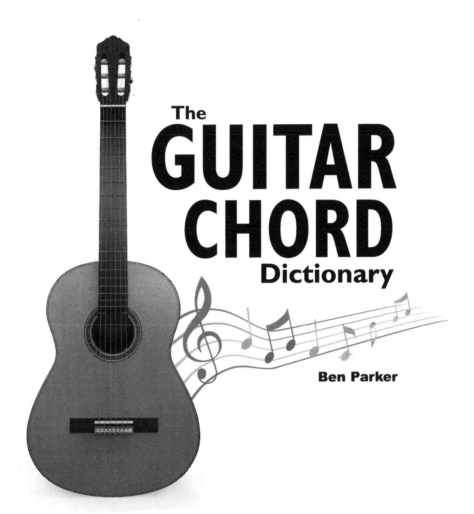

Ben Parker

Author: Ben Parker

Editor: Alison McNicol

First published in 2014 by Kyle Craig Publishing

This version updated Dec 2014

Text and illustration copyright © 2014 Kyle Craig Publishing

Design: Julie Anson

Music set by Ben Parker using Sibelius software

ISBN: 978-1-908707-39-0

A CIP record for this book is available from the British Library.

A Kyle Craig Publication

www.kyle-craig.com

Contents

Introduction

Welcome to **The Guitar Chord Dictionary**!

As a guitar player a large percentage of your playing will be chord playing. This book will give you an introduction to the most popular chord types you'll come across when learning to play songs. It may also give you ideas for chords to use in your own compositions.

Chords for each of the 12 keys are shown in this book. Each key will be spread over two pages. The most common flat and sharp keys are shown first, followed by their enharmonic equivalent i.e. C♯ / D♭.

Chords on the guitar are played using 'shapes' which are shown using chord diagrams. There will be a chord diagram and a photograph for each chord.

How To Read Chord Diagrams

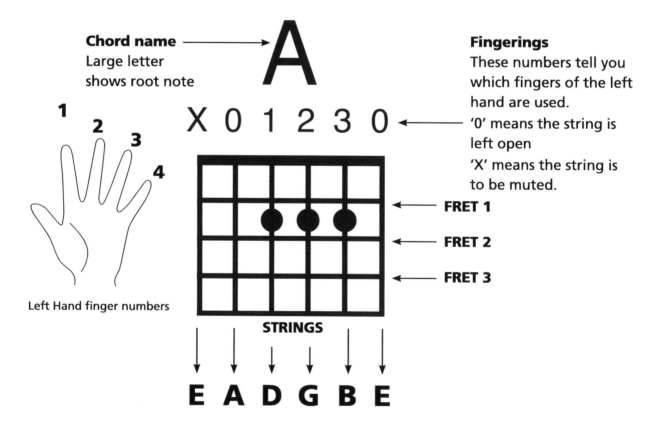

Chord name → **A**
Large letter shows root note

Fingerings
These numbers tell you which fingers of the left hand are used.
'0' means the string is left open
'X' means the string is to be muted.

X 0 1 2 3 0

FRET 1
FRET 2
FRET 3

Left Hand finger numbers

STRINGS

E A D G B E

Left hand fingerings are marked just above each box in line with the string below them. ***PLEASE NOTE*** These are not fret numbers. The dots on the diagram show you which strings and frets to play. The number indicates which of your left hand fingers you should use to push down and fret the note on that string. If the fingering reads '0' then allow that particular string to ring 'open'. When you see an 'X' this means you should try not to play that string as part of

Chords Higher Up The Fretboard

Sometimes it's necessary to play chords higher up the fretboard. This is shown using a fret indication where the word fret is abbreviated to 'fr'.

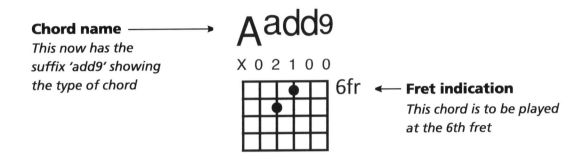

Chord name →
This now has the suffix 'add9' showing the type of chord

Fret indication
This chord is to be played at the 6th fret

Bar Or 'Barre' Chords

Bar chords are when you use the 1st f̸ to fret more than one string by pressing it like a bar across the string̸ ̸ore than one string has the number 1 above it.

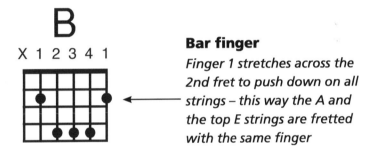

Bar finger
Finger 1 stretches across the 2nd fret to push down on all strings – this way the A and the top E strings are fretted with the same finger

Chord Names Explained

The chord naming convention used in this book is as follows. The numbers below after each chord type represent the notes of the major scale of the key that make up each chord. The notes of the chords in the key of C have been given to clearly illustrate.

THE MAJOR SCALE OF C

C	D	E	F	G	A	B	C	(D)
1	2	3	4	5	6	7	8	(9)

Chord Type	Structure	Spelling in key of C
MAJOR	1 3 5	C E G
MINOR	1 $\flat$3 5	C E$\flat$ G
SEVENTH	1 3 5 $\flat$7	C E G B$\flat$
MINOR SEVENTH	1 $\flat$3 5 $\flat$7	C E$\flat$ G B$\flat$
SUSPENDED 4th	1 4 5	C F G
SUSPENDED 2nd	1 2 5	C D G
MAJOR SEVENTH	1 3 5 7	C E G B
ADDED 9th	1 3 5 9	C E G D

A

X 0 1 2 3 0

A major

Am
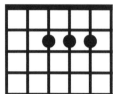
X 0 2 3 1 0

A minor

A⁷
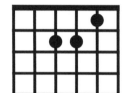
X 0 2 0 3 0

A 7th

Am⁷

X 0 2 0 1 0

A minor 7th

A^{SUS4}

A^{SUS4}

X 0 1 2 3 0

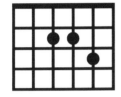

A suspended 4th

A^{SUS2}

X 0 1 2 0 0

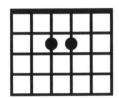

A suspended 2nd

A^{maj7}

X 0 2 1 3 0

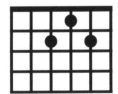

A major 7th

A^{add9}

X 0 2 1 0 0

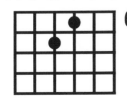 6fr

A added 9th

B♭ / A♯ Chords

B♭

X 1 2 3 4 1

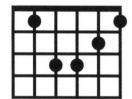

B♭ major

B♭m

X 1 3 4 2 1

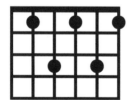

B♭ minor

B♭⁷

X 1 3 1 4 1

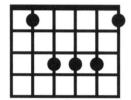

B♭ 7th

B♭m⁷

X 1 3 1 2 1

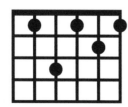

B♭ minor 7th

B♭ / A♯ Chords

B♭SUS2

X 1 3 4 1 1

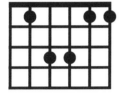

B♭ suspended 2nd

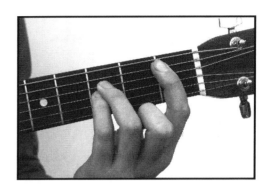

B♭SUS4

X 1 2 3 4 1

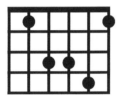

B♭ suspended 4th

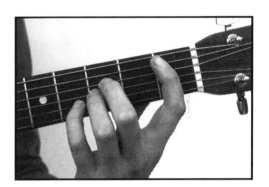

B♭maj7

X 1 3 2 4 1

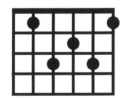

B♭ major 7th

B♭add9

2 X 0 1 3 4

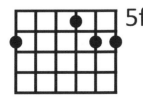
5fr

B♭ added 9th

B
X 1 2 3 4 1

B major

Bm
X 1 3 4 2 1

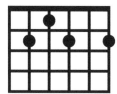

B minor

B⁷
X 2 1 3 0 4

B 7th

Bm⁷
X 1 3 1 2 1

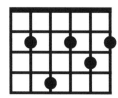

B minor 7th

B^{SUS}4

X 1 3 4 0 0

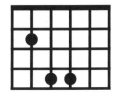

B suspended 4th

B^{SUS}2

X 1 3 4 1 1

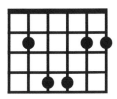

B suspended 2nd

B^{maj}7

X 1 3 2 4 1

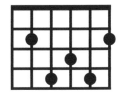

B major 7th

B^{add}9

X 2 1 X 3 4

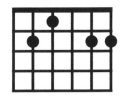

B added 9th

C

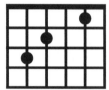

X 3 2 0 1 0

C major

Cm

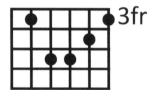

X 1 3 4 2 1

3fr

C minor

C⁷

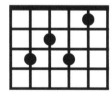

X 3 2 4 1 0

C 7th

Cm⁷

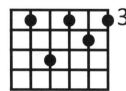

X 1 3 1 2 1

3fr

C minor 7th

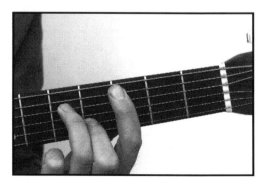

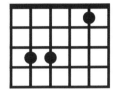

X 3 4 0 1 X

C suspended 4th

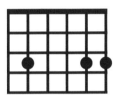

X 2 X 0 3 4

C suspended 2nd

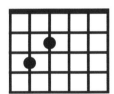

X 3 2 0 0 0

C major 7th

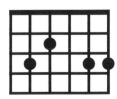

X 2 1 0 3 4

C added 9th

C♯

X 1 2 3 4 1

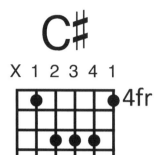

4fr

C♯ major

C♯m

X 1 3 4 2 1

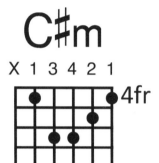

4fr

C♯ minor

C♯7

X 3 2 4 1 X

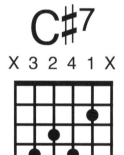

C♯ 7th

C♯m⁷

X 1 3 1 2 1

4fr

C♯ minor 7th

C#sus4

X 3 4 X 1 1

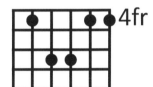

C#suspended 4th

C#sus2

X 1 3 4 1 1   4fr

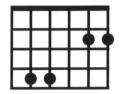

C#suspended 2nd

C#maj7

X 1 3 2 4 1   4fr

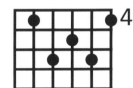

C#major 7th

C#add9

X 2 1 X 3 4

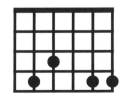

C#added 9th

D

X X 0 1 3 2

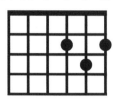

D major

Dm

X X 0 2 3 1

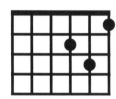

D minor

D⁷

X X 0 2 1 3

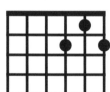

D 7th

Dm⁷

X X 0 2 1 1

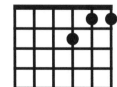

D minor 7th

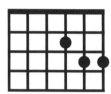

D^{SUS}**4**

X X 0 1 3 4

D suspended 4th

D^{SUS}**2**

X X 0 1 3 0

D suspended 2nd

D^{maj}**7**

X X 0 1 1 1

D major 7th

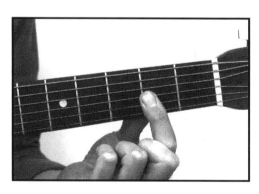

D^{add}**9**

X X 0 3 4 0   7fr

D added 9th

E♭

X 3 2 0 1 4   4fr

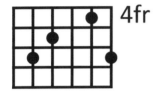

E♭major

E♭m

X X 3 2 4 1

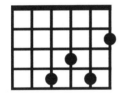

E♭minor

E♭⁷

X X 1 3 2 4

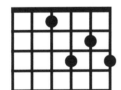

E♭ 7th

E♭m⁷

X X 1 4 2 3

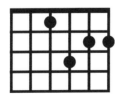

E♭minor 7th

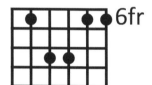

X X 1 2 3 4

**E♭ suspended
4th**

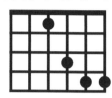

X 1 2 3 4 1 ●6fr

**E♭ suspended
2nd**

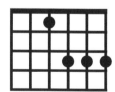

X X 1 2 3 4

E♭ major 7th

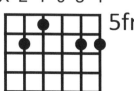

X 2 1 0 3 4 5fr

E♭ added 9th

E

0 2 3 1 0 0

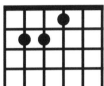

E major

Em

0 1 2 0 0 0

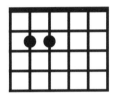

E minor

E⁷

0 2 0 1 0 0

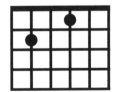

E 7th

Em⁷

0 1 2 0 3 0

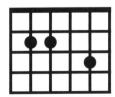

E minor 7th

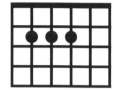

0 2 3 4 0 0

E suspended 4th

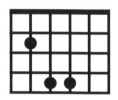

0 1 3 4 0 0

E suspended 2nd

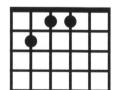

0 3 1 2 0 0

E major 7th

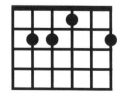

0 2 3 1 0 4

E added 9th

F

X X 4 3 1 2

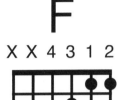

F major

Fm

X X 4 1 2 X

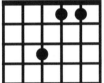

F minor

F⁷

X X 1 4 2 3

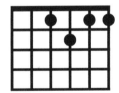

F 7th

Fm⁷

1 3 1 1 1 1

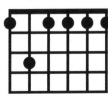

F minor 7th

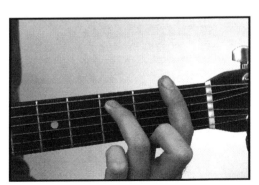

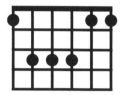 **Fsus4**

1 2 3 4 1 1

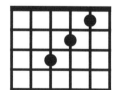 **Fsus2**

X X 3 0 1 1

F suspended 4th

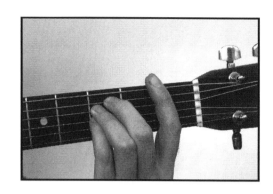

F suspended 2nd

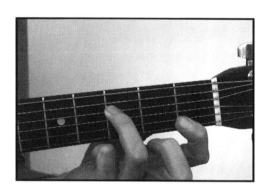

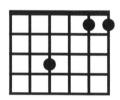 **Fmaj7**

X X 3 2 1 0

F major 7th

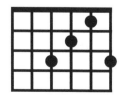 **Fadd9**

X X 3 2 1 4

F added 9th

F♯
X X 4 3 1 2

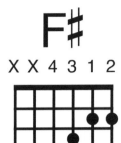

F♯ major

F♯m
X X 4 1 2 X

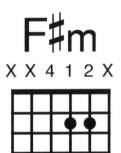

F♯ minor

F♯7
X X 3 2 1 0

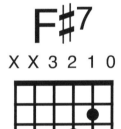

F♯ 7th

F♯m7
1 3 1 1 1 1

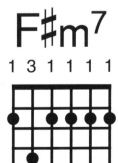

F♯ minor 7th

F♯sus4

1 2 3 4 1 1

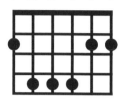

F♯ suspended 4th

F♯sus2

X X 1 3 4 1   4fr

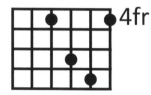

F♯ suspended 2nd

F♯maj7

X X 4 3 2 1

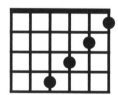

F♯ major 7th

F♯add9

X X 3 2 1 4

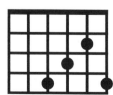

F♯ added 9th

G

2 1 0 0 0 3

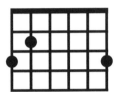

G major

Gm

1 3 4 1 1 1   3fr

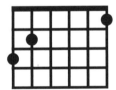

G minor

G⁷

3 2 0 0 0 1

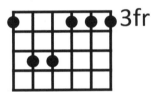

G 7th

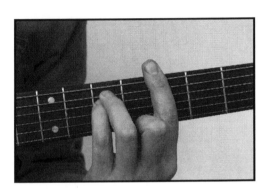

Gm⁷

1 3 1 1 1 1   3fr

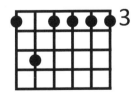

G minor 7th

G^{SUS}4

3 X 0 0 1 4

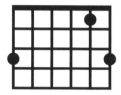

G suspended 4th

G^{SUS}2

2 X 0 1 3 4

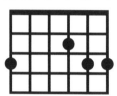

G suspended 2nd

G^{maj7}

3 2 0 0 0 1

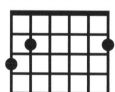

G major 7th

G^{add9}

2 X 0 1 0 3

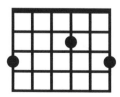

G added 9th

A♭

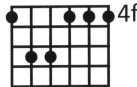
4fr

A♭ major

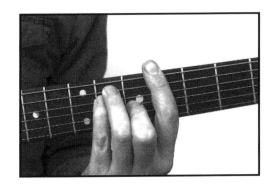

A♭m

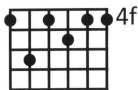
4fr

A♭ minor

A♭⁷

1 3 1 2 1 1
4fr

A♭ 7th

A♭m⁷

1 3 1 1 1 1
4fr

A♭ minor 7th

A♭SUS4

1 2 3 4 1 1
4fr

A♭ suspended 4th

A♭SUS2

2 X X 1 3 4

A♭ suspended 2nd

A♭maj7

X X 4 3 2 1
3fr

A♭ major 7th

A♭add9

X X 3 2 1 4
4fr

A♭ added 9th

MORE GREAT MUSIC BOOKS FROM KYLE CRAIG!

How To Play UKULELE — A Complete Guide for Absolute Beginners

978-1-908-707-08-6

My First UKULELE — Learn to Play: Kids

978-1-908-707-11-6

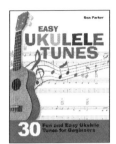

Easy UKULELE Tunes

978-1-908707-37-6

How To Play GUITAR — A Complete Guide for Absolute Beginners

978-1-908-707-09-3

My First GUITAR — Learn to Play: Kids

978-1-908-707-13-0

Easy GUITAR Tunes

978-1-908707-34-5

How To Play KEYBOARD — A Complete Guide for Absolute Beginners

978-1-908-707-14-7

My First KEYBOARD — Learn to Play: Kids

978-1-908-707-15-4

Easy KEYBOARD Tunes

978-1-908707-35-2

How To Play PIANO — A Complete Guide for Absolute Beginners

978-1-908-707-16-1

My First PIANO — Learn to Play: Kids

978-1-908-707-17-8

Easy PIANO Tunes

978-1-908707-33-8

How To Play HARMONICA — A Complete Guide for Absolute Beginners

978-1-908-707-28-4

My First RECORDER — Learn to Play: Kids

978-1-908-707-18-5

Easy RECORDER Tunes

978-1-908707-36-9

How To Play BANJO — A Complete Guide for Absolute Beginners

978-1-908-707-19-2

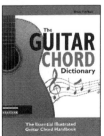

The GUITAR Chord Dictionary

978-1-908707-39-0

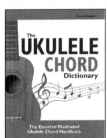

The UKULELE Chord Dictionary

978-1-908707-38-3